Love
Doesn't Ask
Permission

jean piazza

AuthorHouse™
1663 Liberty Drive
Bloomington, IN 47403
www.authorhouse.com
Phone: 833-262-8899

Because of the dynamic nature of the Internet, any web addresses or links contained in this book may have changed since publication and may no longer be valid. The views expressed in this work are solely those of the author and do not necessarily reflect the views of the publisher, and the publisher hereby disclaims any responsibility for them.

Any people depicted in stock imagery provided by Getty Images are models, and such images are being used for illustrative purposes only.
Certain stock imagery © Getty Images.

This book is printed on acid-free paper.

ISBN: 978-1-6655-3296-9 (sc)
ISBN: 978-1-6655-3298-3 (hc)
ISBN: 978-1-6655-3297-6 (e)

Library of Congress Control Number: 2021915082

Print information available on the last page.

Published by AuthorHouse 03/16/2022

authorHOUSE®

I get my power from my words
It's when I say the wrong things
That I am weak

If you can't lead, at least follow correctly

Loving me does not guarantee you a place in my life

The purpose of dreams is to take what you're already
confused about and to confuse you further

I've always been afraid of
something
And I've never known
what it was
And now, I'm afraid of
nothing
But I still don't know what
it was

Once the soul is touched, can it be untouched?

I want to empty all those words from your head.....spilling them onto the bed.....leaving them for dead.....taking you to things not yet said...

People that use others to build themselves up only make themselves look smaller

Your mountain is just higher but that only
means you reach greater heights

Time doesn't stand still no matter how many photos you take

Retrospect sheds
good light

Leave those words where they are

Think of your ego as an enemy. Once you do that, you will be free from your own grip

I thought I heard your voice as the wind blew words through my hair
We were wrong in all the right ways

When it rains, you cannot see your tears
but God can still taste the salt

I love truth

I love how it's not an opinion

Truth does matter
In fact, it makes all the difference

The world
does not
open its
arms to
people like
me so well

If I fix that broken window
Do you think everything will be alright
If I focus on the damage
And not on the light
We placed a window
To open the wall
But it was the force of the inside
That created the fall
You want to blame the window
While I blame the wall
Fixing the window
Does nothing at all

The only way to be prepared for anything in life is
to entertain the possibility of everything

You can't pick and choose the tide....
You can only decide whether or not to ride.....

This is MY life – go find your own

You
You
Touched
My heart
And
I can't
Go back
And with
Everything
That
May never
Be perfect
So much
Just is
Enough

Focus on whether or not you love him, not on whether
or not you can keep him from loving her

I've traveled down many roads
I have passed you going in the
opposite direction
When I looked in my rearview
mirror
I know I saw you looking back
When we locked glances
Our lives only had one direction
No matter what turns or paths
we took
Our lives only had one direction
I was always meant to come back
to you
You were always meant to come
back to me
And although the wind of change
will blow in a new direction
You will forever be with me

I feel like my mind is a piano keyboard and
you know how to play every note

I was going to be cautious when I met you
But you uttered something to me and I left caution behind
As if I had to
I was going to play hard to get
But you touched me and I knew I'd been had
I was going to be coy
But you stared at me and I gave myself away
As if I had to
I was going to be aware
But you smiled at me and I lost touch
I was going to fly away from you
But you asked and you needed and so I will stay
Because I know you love me
As if you had to

I've kept my heart in the place you left it
I know it sits alone
And while I'm trying to accept it
You've gone from cold to stone
There's no comfort in knowing I came the closest
When you can't let go cause you chose this
Don't know how I could have done any better
You gave me too little to work with
I'm aching with this failure
But I never blame you
Learning to love and lose
Not what I would choose
Memories I never realized I was making haunt me
What did you do with yours?
Words engraved
What did you do with yours?
Love made
To fade
What did you do with yours?
Everything is just passing me
Seems like nothing matters
Each moment spins out of control
Feels like nothing can hold me in place

It is not in your best interest to suffer the rest of your life

The problem with forever is that everyone thinks it's forever

Recovering from lower standards
is harder than maintaining
high standards

Saw the full moon again
tonight
Thought of you again
tonight
It's you against the
universe
The battle you rehearse
You're my movement
You're my star
All that I can see
In a dark sky
Thought of you again
tonight
Dancing on the moon

If fate exists, can there ever be a wrong time?

Time is nature's way of keeping everything
from happening all at once

They say no two snowflakes are alike
But I'm not sure
Because I don't think they looked at them all
Yeah, I'm not sure
And they say this love is impossible
But I'm not sure
Because I know they never looked at you and me
Cuz if they did, they'd see
That you are every breath I breathe
Our souls lost till our paths crossed

You're the softness in my life
In a world so very harsh
All the walls I build
Were never meant for you

And no one can explain
How love causes so much pain
What we lose just to gain
And how we're never the same

I did everything unconditionally
But somehow you still owe me
What you gave wasn't free
And it's still costing me

Went to his house as a ghost in the dark
Like to have visions that way
They told me my soul had been sold as some art
Knew that it never would stay
Prayed to a god that has very bad hearing
Didn't want him to hear anyway
Cuz you hear my voice in the absence of silence
When I don't even know what to say

Let my absence serve as the appearance I wish to make

I want life to stand still while I
remember everything about you

If you needed more than my flesh
You could've called me second-best
Instead you put me to the test
And I'm failing you

I haven't got a clue what to do next
But I'm still able to put it down
While you're out messing around
But that's not what I wanted to do

I used to have all the things I wanted
Till I met you
Now the things I have
Exist with no meaning
Because of you
This place is black, white and grey
And I can not erase it

It was the last time that I hurt you
That changed you into something new
That I'm not used to
I asked for it anyway
In my own way

You were the only one who took me seriously
You were so honest with me
Always saw through me
Even knew when to leave me

Uncover me like you used to
When all I did was follow you
And the moon played second fiddle
To your riddle
I'm long past the ages
Of illicit love and sages
Take me to a place
Where you can move me

And those voices don't concern me
All those fingers pointing at me
You got to believe, I really don't care
If doing it all wrong makes me happy
Who can really stop me
And if being myself is the crime
I'm just gonna commit it again
I own my regrets
I'm not taking any bets
Cuz you got to believe
I really don't care

How much time is left
Nobody knows
And I'm not one to count and stare
Why waste a moment on that
There are faster ways to get nowhere

Just a dream that never had a chance
Lovers' oath and final dance
Who do we blame when the heart takes aim
If pride is supposed to keep me in place
It's not a job that I can face
The demons that possess you
Have the power to undress you
It's a fine line between love and hate
But you discovered that too late

Uncover me like you used to
When all I did was follow you
And the moon played second fiddle
To our riddle
I'm long past the ages
Of illicit love and sages
Take me to a place
Where you can move me

Keep a part of you for only you
Never give all of yourself
You never know when you're going to need you

Maybe the world will never understand
what the universe has always known

But I need your arms wrapped around me
I need you breathing down my neck
I need your scent
I need the warmth of your skin pressed
against me
I need your touch
I need the whisper of your voice saying you
love me
I need to ask for too much
And then say it's not enough...
Never enough

You told me I wasn't crazy when I knew I was insane
I didn't want to tell you
But you already understood
And when I hid my tears you wiped them away
And this is everything you want me to forget
But it doesn't go away
Now I don't know where you are
Or how I got here
I remember pacing when I couldn't stand
And you asked me what I was doing
I'm doing the same thing now
I have no answers
I'm insane

I want to be ONE
I don't want to be half of two as one

It doesn't matter to me what you think
What matters to me is how I feel about what you think

Hiding the past in a book of dreams
That I'm gonna sell to a broken world

If it looks like a human,

walks like a human,

talks like a human....

It could still be a sociopath

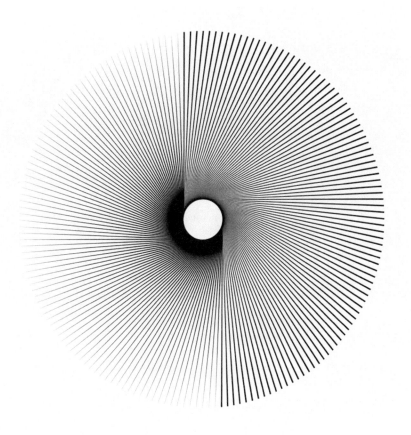

Sometimes the best advice you can get is from an idealist

The phrase "meant to be"
Everybody uses it like it's some magical formula for explaining things
What the fuck is meant to be anyway?
Meant to be is the same as wasn't meant to be

What you have written is basically being undermined by your own pen

So this is what the end feels like
When it's not filled with regrets
And only memories live on
Branding me like a prisoner

I've got to get through this
You made your mark
I don't know if it's in ink
I'm going to find out soon

Threw out all the printed words
All the material objects
Threw out every moment of truth
Trying to empty my memory now

You can either have the pain of losing
Or the pain of never having anything to lose
In either case, you lose
There is no choice but to love

Trying to figure out how to swallow this music so it becomes part of my body and mind

Love should make a coward of a person
It's the most powerful force in the universe
And if you are not afraid of it, it can own you

Baby, I can make the world revolve around me...
It might only be for ten seconds but yea...it will be all about me

All the time that's supposed to heal
Hasn't touched a moment left by you still

I loved you when I met you
I loved you when I knew you
I loved you when you left me
I love you still today

Even in the middle of this new life... life without you
Sometimes the moments stab me and bring me back
When you surrounded all my space with love
God, I miss you

If silence is a language
Then only emptiness
can be heard
You've inspired your
deafening word
In the stillness of this hell
I travel the distance
I know well

Made a decision today
I won't go on this way

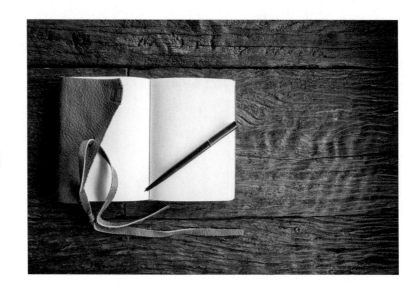

Its not the things that you do to me.....
It's the things that you do to me
When you don't know what you're doing to me
It's not the way you look at me
It's the way you see me
Even without looking
It's not the way you make me feel
It's the way I can't help but feel when I'm with you
It's not the way that you say I love you
It's the way that I know you do

I never thought I'd come here - but here I am
Take my hand in yours... And never let go
It's crazy - I just needed to see you
Someday... Somewhere... Somehow... We will be
together
It has to be my reward
Say you believe me
What I feel for you is so real and if I never love
again, I don't care
I've had it all with you
There is nothing more
You are everything

You don't have to tell me anything
Because we know what is between us
We cry at the same hour
We see with the same power
And it's getting stronger, this bond we're making
And it's getting weaker, the past that's breaking
We're both alone except for when we're together
Regardless of promises of forever
And the raging waters will subside
We will no longer push against the tide
I will do whatever it takes to bring you to safe ground
Because, my love, we have been found

Loyalty is not based on who sees - it is based on how you see

When the world stops spinning, that is only the beginning
Of this eternal love
What began on earth only gave birth
To what will live above
I can talk about here and now
And forget about what I cannot see
But I cannot erase
What forever will be

Do you know that if you cry and close your eyes - it doesn't fucking matter?

You said the past is gone
But it's following me
Trying to figure how long
Before its just a memory

But you pleased me
When you stared me down
And if the past is really gone
Why are you still around

You should care about your image and you should
care about the person that you are but you
can't worry about how you are perceived.
You can only control who you are. You can't
control how others see you.
But with any luck, the two views should be fairly closely aligned.

The greatest truths are learned
through suffering

I want to use my
tongue
to explore your soul

The best way to get my attention is to ignore me

I disagree with the idea that idealism is unrealistic

Fucked up looks good on you

The pages of remorse don't exist for me
I never wrote a line in that book

A shady face can't erase the shadows that fall upon it

Am I taking up too much time in your life
Is there some place else you'd rather be
I can move away if you'd like
Anything to make you happy

There's a road up ahead
And I know you travel alone
But if there's anything I've said
You could take it along

And I've seen the sky that you walked right past by
And I've seen the rain that left you in pain
And you say the words that are always in vain
But this time my love, it isn't the same
Caress me now and save us the time
We both know where this road ends.......
This time.......
This time.....
This road ends.....

Did I cause you to cry behind those closed doors
Was it something I said ... something ignored
Words left to rise – words left to fall
Forgive me my words, they're nothing at all

And when the clouds give way
To the memories that stay
There isn't a chance that I wouldn't take
To give back the trust and all that's at stake

And I've seen the sky that you walked right past by
And I've seen the rain that left you in pain
And you say the words that are always in vain
But this time my love, it isn't the same
Caress me now and save us the time
We both know where this road ends.......
This time.......this time
This road ends

I don't need other people to validate me - I'm self approved

I'm not asking you to love me - I'm asking you why you can't love

I don't want someone to take care of me – I
want someone who cares about me

I'm not good with numbers but I think I'm one person

Designer shirts absorb tears just like cheap cotton

I go back in time
Where I can spend time with you
The places that you took me to
When time had nothing better to do
Sometimes the truth does not free you
When you're an exception to every rule
And when you don't want to be you
There's no one left to fool

But a word can still be perfect
In a line that turns out wrong
And for all that is eclipsed
There's a moment that goes on
What is this reason we cannot see
Who are you if you cannot be
How are we us when we aren't even we
It always comes down to you and me

Can't wait to hear from you
Can't wait for your touch
Can't wait for all the things, baby
That say I miss you so much

Many have measured the distance between us
In miles and in space
But that cannot explain how we came to this place

I don't need to touch you to feel you
I don't need to see you to remember you
I don't need to make love to you to love you

Your words are all I need to be whole
You penetrate my soul
And for all that I may be without
Our love stands with no doubt

It's not written in the stars
And all the choices that I made
Seem so out of place
I see your voice
I hear your face
And my heart is somewhere in between
Now and forever
And I fear I'm going down

I wasn't born to love you
I tell my soul that
I try telling my heart that
Without skipping a beat
You don't want to remember
The words I can't forget
I don't want to remember
Everything you regret

I wanted more time with you
Somehow it was taken away
And I know nothing I can say
Will ever make you stay
There would never have been a right time to lose you
I'm glossing over the details
That feeling in my throat grips me
I'm waiting for the day when it goes away
Not today – not today

And if you only knew what I'm still going through
Damn the time that stands still
They say you have to play to win
They don't say what you pay to lose
And my heart is somewhere in between
Now and forever
I wasn't born to love you
But I sure want to

How can you be that there
And not there at all

I have a scene in my head
It contains the words you said
I cannot say them out loud
I was beautiful
I was high on us
And the smile that emerged was made of you
All the things you say and do
Haven't left me like they've left you
But I love farther than that
Farther than anyone should
And I don't mind being alone
Except for when I do

I've been holding on to something that's gone
While you've been letting go, yea this I know
If pride is supposed to keep me in place
It's not a job I want to face
Cause I'm still falling apart
Underneath this lace

I hear people talk about you
It still takes its toll
I"m left wondering how long I'll have to pay
For loving you this way
Who do we blame when the heart takes aim
What made it so we weren't the same
I'm screaming your name in vain
Guess I'm comfortable living in pain

I've been holding on to something that's gone
While you've been letting go, yea this I know
If pride is supposed to keep me in place
It's not a job I want to face
Cause I'm still falling apart
Underneath this lace

I cannot explain what you are capable of understanding

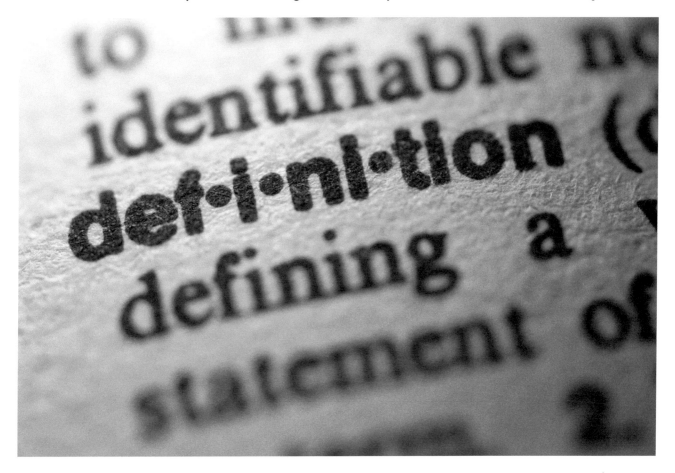

You didn't expect me to lose my way
To make any mistakes
It doesn't surprise me to say
I always knew you'd be wrong
How did I lose so much
If I never had anything
How did I feel the rush
When pain was all it could bring
I'd make every excuse all over again
Because you haven't caused me to regret a thing
I want to be there when you change your mind
But just like you said to me
There's no guarantee

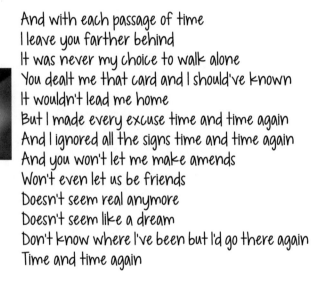

And with each passage of time
I leave you farther behind
It was never my choice to walk alone
You dealt me that card and I should've known
It wouldn't lead me home
But I made every excuse time and time again
And I ignored all the signs time and time again
And you won't let me make amends
Won't even let us be friends
Doesn't seem real anymore
Doesn't seem like a dream
Don't know where I've been but I'd go there again
Time and time again

The way it should be is never too good to be true

It's a dream that never had a chance
Lover's oath and final dance
I've always been the riddle
That you couldn't shake
Now I'm the love you couldn't take
Just a mistake

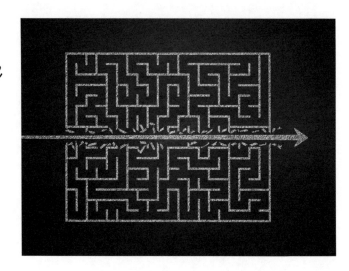

I said I'd be okay no matter the way
We left and grew apart
I said I'd be okay cause I thought I would
But that's not the way it is

And I don't want to tell you
I'm not okay
I don't want to say it's true
I promised I'd always find a way
To be as strong as you
But that's not the way it is
No, I can't make it true
No matter what I do
It's just not the way it is

And I don't want to believe that you're okay
I don't want to know you're gone
I don't want to make my promise pay
For all of the words gone wrong

But that's just the way it is

If you were a different person then, that
makes me a different person now
because I fell in love with who you were

Can you go find yourself privately please?

It's a crazy fucking world but somebody's got to live in it

Do you think justifying stupidity makes you smarter?

There is too much to know so there's no point in imagining what does not exist

Every shadow I slip in and out of
You adjust
When I need your voice
When I don't
You adjust
No questions
You just adjust
You've stayed when I thought there was no reason
You knew what I didn't know
And now I understand
You love me

How do you not notice who you are?

Ignoring something is the same thing as saying something
It's just harder to decipher

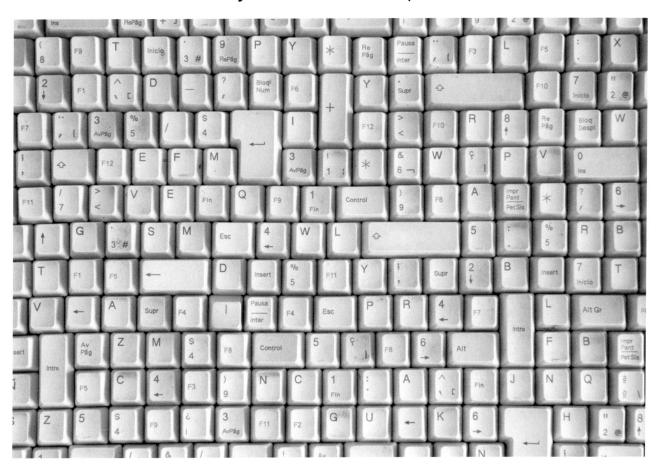

I've never been anyone's wrong decision

I know it's early
But the last time
It was too late
So I just want to tell you now
I love you

Never put yourself in a position you can't get out of

I will make you remember everything you never knew you forgot

I woke up this morning and realized I hadn't thought about you
But then it was too late

You say I ask very hard questions but you don't know how hard they are for me to ask

If you have to ask yourself whether you trust someone?
You don't

Does it feel right
Because I don't know how it can
Without me being totally wrong
And I've never felt more right about
anyone in my life

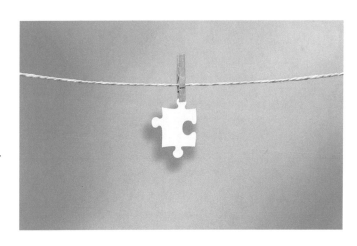

Saying you love me too much is like saying you can shortchange the universe and you can't

No one owes you anything but you owe yourself everything

When what you have is what you had, what do you actually have?

A memory

It's not what you put me through
It's what you needed to go through

No matter what you discover in this universe,
just know that you have unearthed me

I've thought about wanting you
About you touching me
And then I stop
As if I can't handle it
I've thought about your
lips touching mine
I've imagined it
But I can't imagine it

I've thought about your hand
Slipped in mine
And that would be all I could feel
All I would be aware of
Your hand in mine

I've wondered what
you've thought about
And then I stop
I've thought about the words
I love you
But that's so far
Do you say them
I've said them
It's so simple what I want
A single touch
An inch of the universe unveiled
Revealed
Glance at me
Just see me
Don't make me ask
Because I probably won't

You cannot create order where chaos is preferred

Can you teach me how to play chess
I want to know how you think
I want to pretend I'm not
watching your every move
When you know I am
I'm afraid to look away
Or miss a word you don't say
I don't know if I'm ever
going to sleep again

I did cry once
And haven't stopped since
And you still make me happier
than I've ever been
But I'm so sad all the time
Teach me how to cope
In a world of isolation
Teach me how to pray

What would it be like had I never known you
Teach me how to pray
These are my hands
I know how to touch you
My heart hasn't been any place for so long
I don't think you have any idea
how much I love you
Your tears aren't tears to me
They are drops of music that help you see
Teach me how to listen
So I don't miss a beat
Teach me how to see through you
Teach me how to play chess

You cannot taste something that you've already swallowed

It's not the way you thought
It's not the color of life
Makes you wonder why
The world doesn't seem right

You're still an angel in my eyes
I'm not daunted by your pain
If I could erase what you feel
Return what you can't claim

Don't ask a child to be brave
Don't take away a chance to cry
If you need to fall apart
Let me be the one to stand close by

Don't ask a child to be brave
It's not what you would decide
But chance and fate stand alone
Until the moment they collide

The shadow never leaves you
Although it changes size
But from every view I see you
The teardrops in your eyes

It's not the way you thought
But somehow it is right
What you can't make sense of
Comes from another light

Don't ask a child to be brave
Don't take away a chance to cry
If you need to fall apart
Let me be the one to stand close by

Don't ask a child to be brave
It's not what you would decide
But chance and fate stand alone
Until the moment they collide

There are things that happen to you and then there are things that you allow to happen to you

Your heart is
breathing words
Your voice so seductive
And I am completely
captured
By the light inside you

We are artists
We cover every surface
Every layer

When you're down for no reason whatsoever or happy
for every reason in the world...share it with me

People love the concept of "I'll do it later"
Later is now if you look at it sooner

This moment when my world is perfect
This moment that won't last forever
Now and forever always at odds
This moment when I wish I didn't know any better

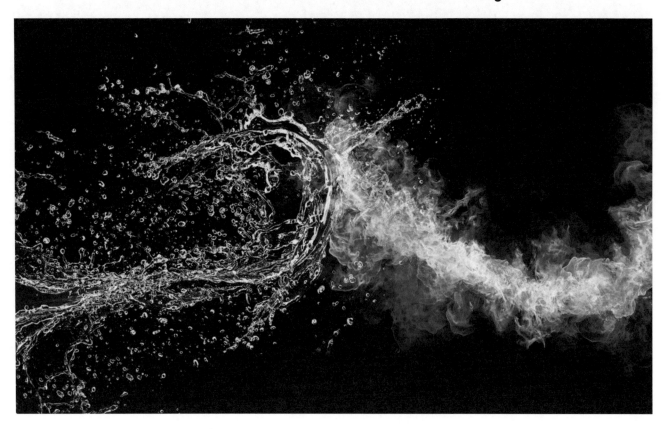

Sometimes I see your face
And I think I can push back
And get past what I can't get past
Just forget all that went wrong
Start this whirlwind over
I wanted to fall in love with you
But you were already in love with yourself
Somehow you had me believe
There was room for me
I never found that space

Tears are just drops of life's lessons – may you have many

Pain, although it's a quiet emotion, leaves the loudest scars

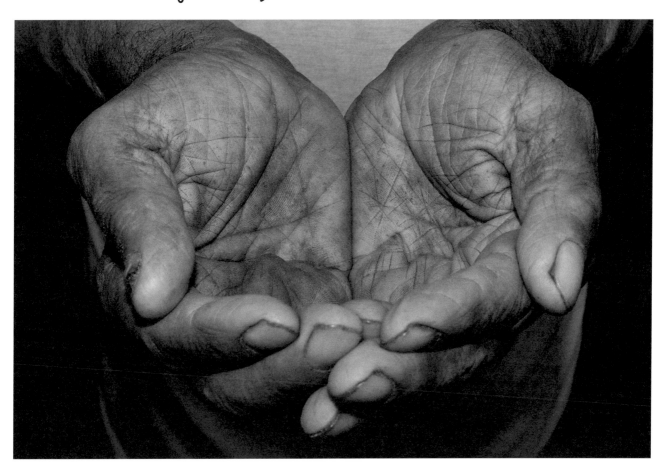

When reality hits, it's never the same as a runaway imagination

If I say not enough
If I say too much
If I say nothing at all
If I just cave and let the words fall
Does it count in the end
Who will recognize the hours
Who will say its all been worth it
How many mistakes to make it perfect

Fade in fade out
Never landing
Expanding my strength for everyone
I carried the years
Thinking I knew something about a pay off
Now I'm way off course
When a dream doesn't end
No matter how many changes I make
Why can't I read the written words

And then you
And then you
Out of nowhere
Make sense to me
Out of nowhere set me free
I've been empty
For so long
Each tomorrow visits yesterday
I have to take something for myself eventually
Do it without the guilty

Trace me trace you
And then you
Trace me tracing you
And then you
Out of nowhere
Make sense to me
Make me face me
Without the guilty
And then you
And then you
Remind me about me

It's my fault
For thinking it could be anything other than what it wasn't

Just because someone wears a mask
Doesn't mean you have to perform the great unveiling

I dreamt about you
I dreamt you cared
That's how I know it was a dream

Most people don't listen
They're too busy waiting to talk

I don't need anyone's love more than my own

I don't judge myself according to your standards

Some people become famous to show the world who they are

Some people become stars and change what
the world is because of who they are

Like a world without color, I adapted to you
Saw all the grey without any hue
We were over long before we were through
And that was all okay with you

So I don't know why you ask me
Why you haven't seen me cry
You never deserved the best of me
And tears would be a lie

I don't know why you ask me
How I can just move on
When I never stood still with you
We were always wrong

Does your soul look different in person

It's terribly sad
When you touch something that means everything
And yet nothing comes of it

I don't let small minds create less space in mine

What is your excuse?

How would you survive when put to the test
Would you turn your face like the rest

Imagine if sleep really worked
And I could actually forget
And the morning wasn't a curse
And the day wasn't a lie
A lie I cannot even rehearse

Don't turn the light on
There's nothing to see here
I don't know the way that it was
I don't remember anything before this
Don't turn the light on
You don't want to see this

And I don't know when the struggle began
I don't know how long I've been alone
But it's never going to be the same
You can't go back to a place you never came from
You can't go back to a place you've never been

Don't say a word
There's nothing to hear now
No one hears the heart pound
Not even words have sound
Don't say a word
Silence has taken me down

As long as you're looking, you'll be ok
It's the people who don't even know that there's something to look
for that are in trouble
As they say, ignorance is bliss but it ain't no bliss of mine

When the world was perfect
With all of its flaws
When I chose not to know better
Studying your paws
You never knew all of my fears
And you've been spared all of my tears
Not a night goes by
That I do not cry
That I do not feel for the empty space where you once did lie
There's not a puppy that could ever replace
And oh, what I'd give to kiss your face

Printed in the United States
by Baker & Taylor Publisher Services